Medway
COUNCIL

Serving You

Library	**JUNIOR**	
Telephone: 01634 337799		
21/9/18	24 AUG 2023	
2 9 OCT 2018		
21/12/20		
1 8 FEB 2020		
3 1 OCT 2020		
1 7 JUL 2021		
0 9 AUG 2021	WITHDRAWN	
1 6 AUG 2021		
1 5 SEP 2022		

Books should be returned or renewed by the last date
stamped above.

CW00973003

MEDWAY LIBRARIES

9560000114497

Being a Butterfly

ANNABELLE LYNCH
LUCY DAVEY

WAYLAND
www.waylandbooks.co.uk

First published in Great Britain in 2018 by Wayland.

Illustrations copyright © 2018 by Lucy Davey
Text copyright © 2018 by Hodder and Stoughton

All rights reserved.

Wayland, an imprint of
Hachette Children's Group
Part of Hodder and Stoughton
Carmelite House
50 Victoria Embankment
London
EC4Y 0DZ

An Hachette UK Company
www.hachette.co.uk
www.hachettechildrens.co.uk

ISBN 978 1 5263 0640 1
10 9 8 7 6 5 4 3 2 1

Printed and bound in China

Design by Anthony Hannant
(Little Red Ant)
Edited by Julia Bird

Medway Libraries and Archives

95600000114497	
Askews & Holts	
Cha	£12.99

FSC
MIX
Paper from responsible sources
FSC® C104740
www.fsc.org

Contents

Left on a leaf

In the shade of a big, leafy tree fluttered a bright blue butterfly. She circled a leaf, then landed and rested for a moment, opening her delicate wings wide.

Then she fluttered her wings again, and was gone.

But now on the leaf there sat a
tiny, round white egg.

Hatching out

The little egg stayed on the leaf for ten days. It clung on through wind and rain and sunny days. It swayed in the breeze and basked in warm, golden sunshine. It was sniffed by dogs, spied on by birds and buzzed around by busy bees.

Then, one warm summer morning, the little egg suddenly **twitched**.

Then the little egg twitched again. Then it **shook**.

Suddenly there was a little...**POP!**

The egg shell cracked open. Bit by bit, out came a tiny, fuzzy, green caterpillar.

A greedy caterpillar

The tiny caterpillar **crawled** slowly
along the leaf until she reached a
plump, juicy bud.

She burrowed into the bud and began to **eat** and **eat**...and **eat!**

At last, the caterpillar's belly was full.

She nestled against a leaf, where her fuzzy green skin helped to keep her hidden from hungry birds and insects.

9

Shedding skin

The little caterpillar wasn't quite so little any more.
After a few days, her skin began to feel a bit snug.
She crawled under a nearby leaf. There, she started
to moult, or peel off, her skin. Underneath, the
little caterpillar had soft, new green skin.
The old skin made a tasty snack!

The little caterpillar moulted three more times over the next few days. Now she was **much** bigger and had purple markings. She was also fully grown.

Time to sleep

The caterpillar was
ready for a long rest. She inched down the
stem of a plant, where she would be safe in the
shade of some leaves. There, she spun a fine
silk string to attach herself to
the ground.

Then the caterpillar moulted one last time.
This time, instead of fuzzy green skin, she
was covered in a soft brown case.

After a day or two, the case grew hard, ready to keep the caterpillar safe.

Time to cha**ng**e

The caterpillar stayed snug inside her chrysalis all through the long, cold winter. Big changes were happening to the little caterpillar.

Very slowly, her body broke down and began to change shape. She grew six long, bendy legs, big eyes and spiky antennae. Two silky wings sprouted from her back.

A beautiful butterfly

One warm morning in early spring, a crack appeared in the chrysalis.

First a spindly antenna, then a head emerged from the chrysalis, followed by a body with two soft wings.

The little caterpillar had become a **beautiful** butterfly!

She shrugged off the remains of her chrysalis and perched on a nearby leaf, beating her silvery-blue wings fast.

Learning to fly

At first, the butterfly's wings were too small and damp for her to fly. She began pumping blood through her wings to help them grow bigger and stronger. The warm sunshine helped to dry the butterfly's wings.

At last, the butterfly was ready to fly.

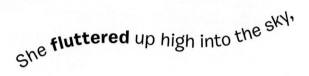

She **fluttered** up high into the sky,

tumbling and **twirling** through the air.

Finding flwers

Flying was hard work! The butterfly was soon ready to rest and to eat. She perched daintily on the edge of a leaf, next to some sweet-smelling purple flowers.

To eat, she rolled out a long tube, called a proboscis, from her mouth.

Then she planted her proboscis in the middle of a flower and sucked up its delicious nectar.

After her sweet snack, the butterfly was ready to take flight again.

21

Busy butterflies

As the days grew longer and warmer, the park was soon filled with fluttering butterflies.

Some were **big**, some were small.

Some were brightly coloured, others were white as snow.

22

Some had **dots**...   ...others had **stripes**.

All were busy flying from flower to flower, gathering nectar to eat.

Finding a mate

As the sunny summer days stretched on, it was time for the butterfly to find a mate.

Before long, a bright blue male butterfly fluttered close by.

He spun and twirled high into the sky in a beautiful courtship dance, hoping to attract the butterfly's attention.

She watched for a while, then fluttered up to join him.

The two butterflies came to rest on
a leaf, with their wing tips pressed
close together.

New life

A few days later, the butterfly had a very important job to do. She fluttered busily from leaf to leaf, looking for just the right spot to settle.

26

Finally, she rested on a broad green leaf,
dappled with golden sunshine.

She settled there for an
instant or two, then flew
off again to join the other
butterflies in the bright sky.

But now on the leaf there
sat a tiny, round white egg.

Brilliant butterflies

All butterflies are beautiful, but some butterflies are truly amazing.

The Queen Alexandra Birdwing is the biggest butterfly in the world. The female has wings that measure around 30 centimetres tip to tip. That's as big as a pizza!

The Common Brimstone butterfly camouflages itself as a leaf to fool hungry predators.

Skipper butterflies zoom along at 60 kilometres per hour – as fast as a swallow!

Painted Lady butterflies migrate from Africa to the Arctic! They travel in stages as the butterflies die along the way and are replaced by the next generation – a bit like a relay team.

29

Protecting butterflies

Butterflies make our world a bright, beautiful place. They also help plants to grow and spread by carrying pollen between them. But butterflies are in danger everywhere. Wildflower meadows are disappearing, so butterflies cannot feed. They are also harmed by the chemicals that some farmers spray on their crops.

We can all help to save butterflies. If you have a garden at home, plant some flowers such as lavender or phlox that lots of types of butterflies love to snack on. If not, how about putting some pot plants on your balcony or helping to create a butterfly-friendly garden at school? You will have some beautiful visitors!

Glossary

antennae: The two long, thin parts on an animal's head that it uses to feel things.

bud: A little lump on a tree or plant that will turn into a leaf or flower.

camouflage: When an animal blends in with its surroundings.

chrysalis: The hard case that protects a caterpillar while it turns into a butterfly.

mate: An animal's partner, which it breeds with.

migrate: To travel long distances, usually to feed or breed.

moult: To peel off a covering in order to grow.

nectar: A sweet, sticky liquid made by flowers.

offspring: An animal's young or children.

pollen: A sticky yellow dust produced by flowers.

predator: An animal that eats other animals.

proboscis: A long tube, used for sucking up food.

🔍 Find out more

If you would like to learn more about butterflies, here are some books and websites that can help you:

I-Spy Butterflies and Moths (Collins Michelin, 2018)

Look and Wonder: The Amazing Life Cycle of Butterflies by Kay Barnham (Wayland, 2017)

RSPB First Book of Butterflies and Moths by Derek Riemann (A&C Black, 2012)

Butterfly Conservation is a charity dedicated to protecting butterflies, moths and their habitats. You can also identify butterflies and moths from photos on their website. Find them at butterfly-conservation.org.

Find out more about butterfly's life cycles at **National Geographic's** children's website: natgeokids.com/uk/discover/animals/insects/butterfly-life-cycle/